Hilary's plays include *Fortune, Eye of the Storm, Shot While Dancing, The Falls,* and *The Anatomy Lesson of Doctor Ruysch.* She has written the book and lyrics for a musical, *The Wedding Song,* the libretto for the opera *Mrs. Satan,* and lyrics for the song cycle *Talk Show.* ABC Radio has broadcast *Cruisin', Wreckage, Wolf Lullaby* and *The Anatomy Lesson of Doctor Ruysch,* and has commissioned *Love's Delightful Labours.* She also writes for film and television.

She is a graduate of the National Institute of Dramatic Art, the Australian Film, Television and Radio School, and the Julliard Playwrights' Studio in New York. She is the recipient of the Philip Parsons Young Playwrights' Award, the Aurealis Award for children's literature, the Jill Blewitt Playwrights' Award (for *Wolf Lullaby*) and the Eric Kocher Playwrights' Award.

Photo: Stuart Campbell

For Lucy

Wolf Lullaby

HILARY
BELL

Currency Press • Sydney

CURRENCY PLAYS

First published 1997 by
Currency Press Ltd,
PO Box 2287, Strawberry Hills NSW 2012, Australia
enquiries@currency.com.au, www.currency.com.au
This revised edition first published 2002

Reprinted 2003, 2007, 2009

NATIONAL LIBRARY OF AUSTRALIA CIP DATA
Bell, Hilary, 1966– .
    Wolf lullaby.
    Rev. ed.
    ISBN 978 0 86819 668 8
    1. Juvenile homicide - Drama. 2. Violence in children - Drama. 3. Tasmania - Drama. I. Title.
    A822.3

Printed by Ligare Book Printers, Riverwood
Cover design by Anaconda Graphic Design/Trevor Hood
Cover: Tara Morice as Angela Gael and Lucy Bell as Lizzie Gael in the Griffin Theatre production at the Stables, 1996 (Photograph: Robert McFarlane)

Contents

Lucy Bell as Lizzie in the 1996 Griffin Theatre Company production.
Photo: Robert McFarlane.

Author's Note

HILARY BELL

Wolf Lullaby began life in mid 1993, inspired by a newspaper article about a 13-year-old boy in a small town, who had murdered a 4-year-old. The photograph showed a bewildered red-head, freckles and glasses, being handcuffed before a rabid crowd. It was only a few months after the killing of 2-year-old James Bulger by two 10-year-olds in England. The headlines ('Little Devils', 'Bad Seed', 'Born to Murder', 'Evil, Brutal and Cunning', 'How Do You Feel Now You Little Bastards') were less shocking to me than Prime Minister John Major's response: 'We must begin to forgive less, and condemn more.' It wasn't so much outrage at the hatred turned on these children (for what they did was unspeakable), but at the ease with which a society relieved itself of any responsibility. It was quick to accuse: working-class parents; single, working mothers; TV; genes; lack of moral education by the church and schools... Never once did we turn the mirror back on ourselves, on a society where banal acts of evil are committed every moment. These acts are often minute—and alone, hardly constitute 'evil'. I mean the way we ignore children, neglect them, lie to them because the truth is too complicated or uncomfortable. The gulf between what we demand of them, and our own actions. The abuse—physical, sexual, emotional, psychological—that is perpetrated against many children every day and night. And not just (sometimes not even) parents—but teachers, the media, the community. The true teaching of morality can only be through example, and that requires vigilance of behaviour. By purporting the idea of children being 'born evil', we are simply abdicating societal responsibility. I didn't write the play in order to explain why such an atrocity occurs—who can say? But I believe there are a number of elements which can act on a person, and, should they themselves be unstable, something terrible can happen. Of course, many people go through a hellish childhood and grow up to be saints.

But those less resilient are stunted, and sometimes poisoned. For some child murderers, the fatal blow is a cry for help: absurd as it sounds, it is one sure way of getting the attention they crave.

Then there is the fact of children's natural violence. How many of us can claim as children to have never committed an act of savagery on something—or someone—smaller and weaker? Talking to people during the writing of this play, I was continually astonished by how close so many had come to killing or being killed—and what it was that had stopped them.

The theme of truth and lies also runs deep. How does a child's perception of 'truth' vary from an adult's? Is it more important to a child to report a fact, or to appease an angry parent? What do we do with a child who commits such a crime? To what extent are they responsible, and to what extent are we?

Perhaps the most difficult situation is that faced by the murderer's parents. For those of the victim, the reaction is grief, rage, loss. But for the other parents, there must be a maelstrom of conflicting emotions: Natural love, horror, disgust, fear, loyalty, self-examination, and of course grief, but grief of a kind that is not easy to resolve.

The play evolved, over three years, with invaluable input from many people, not only dramaturgically, but also those who confided in me their own inglorious confessions. I would like to thank all of these, especially the actors, dramaturges and director of the 1994 Australian National Playwrights' Conference, and of the Griffin Theatre Company production.

April 1997

Wolf Lullaby was first produced by Griffin Theatre Company at the Stables Theatre, Sydney on 23 April 1996, with the following cast:

LIZZIE GAEL	Lucy Bell
ANGELA GAEL	Tara Morice
WARREN GAEL	Sean O'Shea
SERGEANT RAY ARMSTRONG	Anthony Phelan

Directed by John O'Hare
Setting designed by Genevieve Blanchett
Lighting designed by Efterpi Soropos
Sound designed by John Hessey
Dramaturge Ros Horin

Production Notes

There are a few tricky demands made in the play, perhaps the greatest of which is how to realise the Wolf. In the first production, directed by John O'Hare, we came up with some solutions that may be useful to future productions. I chose not to put them in the stage directions, because I didn't want to limit the director's imagination. But these notes may prove useful...

The 'transitions', including Scene 8, were spoken by the three actors other than she playing Lizzie. The verses took a quality even more sinister as they slowly encroached on the on-stage action. The first was sung off-stage; the second on the stage's periphery; and in the case of Scene 8, the adults entered and created Lizzie's nightmare, speaking the poem with a 'story-telling' lilt.

The three actors also did Toby's voice in Scene 11. They were all on stage, in semi-darkness, and by dividing the lines between them, Lizzie's fear was augmented as the ghost's voice came from three different directions, surrounding her. They simply stood up and walked out, in semi-darkness, as Lizzie continued the scene with her song.

Our set was dominated by blackboards covered in obsessive chalk graffiti: 'I murder so that I may come back'. In the transition between Scenes 4 and 5, Lizzie lay her (baby-sized) doll on the ground and drew a chalk outline around it, and then lay on that outline, leading into Scene 5.

The Wolf itself was made manifest simply by a sound: A deep rumble, which grew in intensity until it shook the theatre.

Characters

LIZZIE GAEL, 9 years old
ANGELA GAEL, 28, Lizzie's mother
WARREN GAEL, 28, Lizzie's father
SERGEANT RAY ARMSTRONG, 50
CHILDREN'S VOICES
VOICE OF TOBY, a two-year-old.

Setting

Time: The present.
Place: A small industrial town in Tasmania.
Action: The story unfolds over a period of about ten days.
Props and set should be minimal.

Note on Layout

A slash / denotes the following character interrupts while the first
character continues talking.

RAY: The tests on her shoes / were positive –
ANGELA: Yes but what if she didn't?

Acknowledgements

The author's research for this play included reading a wide variety of
newspaper articles on the James Bulger case, the Eric Smith case, the
Mary Bell case and the Jeffrey Dahmer case as well as various
children's rhymes and fairy tales. Gitta Sereny's book, *The Case of
Mary Bell* (London: Arrow Books, 1972) was another very helpful
resource.

SCENE ONE

The wasteland. LIZZIE *plays a game with stones and sticks.*

LIZZIE:

> Ding dong my funeral bell,
> Farewell to my mother.
> Bury me in the old churchyard
> Beside my elder brother.
>
> My coffin shall be white,
> Six white angels by my side,
> Two to sing and two to play
> And two to carry my soul away.

SCENE TWO

The hairdressing salon. ANGELA *cuts* WARREN*'s hair as he reads the paper.* ANGELA *and* WARREN *are good-humoured throughout, if slightly exasperated.* LIZZIE, *doing homework, shouts above the radio.*

LIZZIE: Guess what?

> *She waits.*

Mum? One more day of school. Then it's Christmas Eve! Dad, will you come to our place for Christmas? And then it's the holidays, I can wash their hair for you! You should've seen all the animals we had. Andy brought his fish in a cornflake box and it died. Samantha brought three chihuahuas and she's got even more at home. She's got about seven. She collects them. How do you spell chihuahua?

> *Pause.*

Mum?

ANGELA: Do you think we could have five minutes' silence? Please?

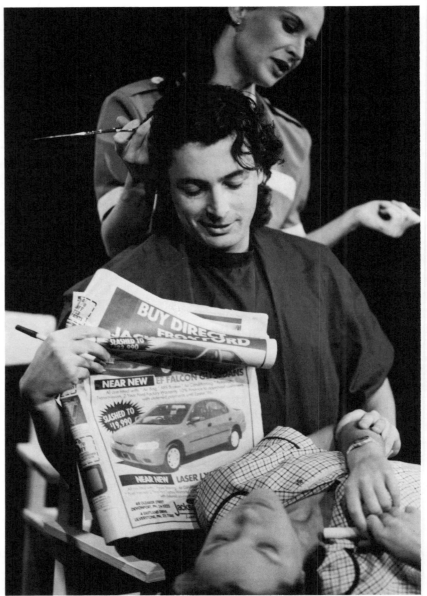

Tara Morice as Angela and Sean O'Shea as Warren in the 1996 Griffin Theatre production. Photo Robert McFarlane.

WARREN: How much you taking off?!

ANGELA: You had knots.

LIZZIE: How many minutes left?

ANGELA: Four and a half.

LIZZIE: I have to spell it right, or I'll get busted.

> ANGELA *cuts.* WARREN *reads the paper.*

Mum, can you show me how to do that?

WARREN: Not on my hair you won't.

ANGELA: The scissors are too sharp for you. When you're older. [*To* WARREN] So what about Christmas? You doing anything?

WARREN: I'll come over. If I'm invited, that is.

> ANGELA *laughs.*

LIZZIE: Norman brought his two budgies. Can I take Tweetie in next Pet Day?

WARREN: That's your mum's bird. You can get your own bird, love.

LIZZIE: [*pointing to the newspaper*] Who's she?

WARREN: A politician.

LIZZIE: What did she do wrong?

WARREN: Darling, I'm trying to read.

ANGELA: Two minutes. Can we handle that?

> LIZZIE *wanders around the room.*

Don't touch anything.

> LIZZIE *sits by* ANGELA*'s legs.*

Ow!

> WARREN *too reacts, stabbed by the scissors.*

WARREN: Christ!

ANGELA: She's pulling the hairs out! Lizzie!

WARREN: We'll ignore you. Is that what you want? 'Cause that's what you're asking for.

ANGELA: Sit there and do your work.

> *She obeys.*

LIZZIE: There was a dog-fight between one of them chihuahuas and Mr Muir's sausage dog. We had to put one in the drawer. It was my job to see all the animals had drinks of water and to fill them up with the hose.

WARREN: [*indicating the paper*] That's not bad: four forty-nine dollars.

ANGELA: What for?

WARREN: Windscreen tinting.

ANGELA: Shop around.

LIZZIE: I like animals. Do you? Do you, Mum and Dad?

WARREN: Foy's cost you upward of four eighty. At least.

ANGELA: Highway robbery.

LIZZIE: I think they're great. I wish I was one. What would you be? Dad?

WARREN: [*taking the mirror*] Let me see. Gawd, woman.

LIZZIE: I'd be something cuddly. Something cute that you could pick up and kiss and stroke. Something small. A guinea pig. Do you think maybe I could get a guinea pig? Would you get me one as a present? Because I haven't asked for anything for ages. Just something little to snuggle.

LIZZIE *looks in* WARREN's *mirror, plays with* ANGELA's *hair.*

But you can squeeze too tight. They shouldn't be so small.

ANGELA: Get the Saturday papers. They'll have specials.

LIZZIE: It's bad to make them so small.

WARREN: Even do it myself. You can buy the stuff in sheets, just stick it on.

LIZZIE: I wish I was the smallest, with the smallest hands. Dad?

WARREN: Terry did it himself. Stuffed it up of course, but he's a git, isn't he? Wouldn't ask him to help.

ANGELA: You're better off getting it done.

WARREN: Cost you three times as much.

ANGELA: Customers notice, wrinkles in the tinting. I'd get a professional. [*Fluffing his hair*] There you go.

WARREN: You're beaut. When are you out of here?

ANGELA: Soon as I clean up.

WARREN *makes to go. Then he remembers* LIZZIE.

WARREN: Hey, Liz. How'd you reckon the girls'll like my haircut?

LIZZIE *mimics him. The three of them laugh.*

See you Christmas Day, then.

He kisses LIZZIE *and exits.* ANGELA *tidies as she talks.*

ANGELA: Next Thursday night shopping we'll go to the mall. Find Dad's present, chocolates or something. And a nice card. You can choose.

LIZZIE: Chocolates!

ANGELA: Now it's time to lock up.

CHILDREN: [*off*]
You know last night,
You know the night before,
Three little tomcats came knocking at the door.
One had a fiddle,
The other had a gun,
The third had a pancake stuck to his bum.

Early in the morning,
Early in the morning,
Early in the morning,
Before the break of day.

SCENE THREE

A cell. Darkness. The clang of the cell door opening as RAY *switches on the light to reveal* LIZZIE.

RAY: Have a good look around. Go on. Not very nice, is it? No TV, no mattress. No comics. That big door with no window. When you go to sleep, do you have a light on? Get frightened in the dark? Well it gets very dark in here.

Pause.

I hear you've been a bad girl, Elizabeth.

LIZZIE: [*whispering*] 'Lizzie'.

RAY: What?

LIZZIE: [*inaudibly*] My mum and dad call me that.

RAY: You'll have to speak up.

She murmurs.

Your mum and dad call you 'Lizzie', do they? Well I'm not your mum and dad. And if you carry on like you have been, you might not see them again for a very long time. How old are you?

LIZZIE: [*whispering*] Nine.

RAY: When will you be ten?

LIZZIE: [*whispering*] I don't know.

RAY: You don't know. Do you know why you're in trouble? On the last day of school?

LIZZIE: I can't spell chihuahua.

RAY: You know the difference between truth and lies?

> *Barely perceptibly,* LIZZIE *nods.*

You do. What happens to little girls who lie?

> LIZZIE *murmurs.*

They go to hell, do they?

> LIZZIE *nods.*

You've told lies in the past, haven't you? Now come off it. Don't start with that smiling again. You are quite capable of telling lies. Convincing lies, aren't you? You tell me why you think you're here.

LIZZIE: [*whispering*] Don't know.

RAY: The shop detective called me in. It's not the first time, either. She says you went pinching things from Coles.

> LIZZIE *shakes her head.*

I don't think a detective would lie, but I think you might.

> LIZZIE *shakes her head.* RAY *takes texta colours from his pocket.*

What's this, then? You haven't got the money for these.

> LIZZIE *murmurs.*

Your lunch money? I don't think so. What's more, you wagged school to do it, didn't you? *Didn't you?* I spoke to your teacher. So you're not only a truant, you're also a thief. Not looking good, is it? You going to be a regular visitor here?

> LIZZIE *whispers.*

I don't care if Errol Nugent's got them. If your mum wanted you to have texta colours, she'd buy them.

Sean O'Shea as Warren and Lucy Bell as Lizzie in the 1996 Griffin Theatre production. Photo Robert McFarlane.

Pause.

And now perhaps you'd like to tell me about Pet Day.

LIZZIE *looks at him.*

Yesterday. What happened to the budgerigars, Elizabeth?

LIZZIE *murmurs.*

Nothing? Oh, I don't think 'nothing' happened at all.

He takes two dead birds from his other pocket.

Little Johnny Whatsit doesn't call this 'nothing'. Thanks to you, that's a very sad boy. You wait till everyone's gone to play-lunch, then you sneak inside and strangle them.

LIZZIE: [*whispering*] I never.

RAY: Well they don't look very alive to me. So what does *that* make you?

LIZZIE *is silent.*

How could you do such a horrible thing? Twist their necks?

LIZZIE: The wolf.

Beat.

RAY: I'm going to have to teach you a lesson, Miss Gael. I don't want to, but it seems to be the only way to get it through your thick skull: be naughty, and you get *in trouble.*

He reaches for the light.

LIZZIE: Don't switch the light out, please sir.

RAY: Well what about that? I was starting to think you had no tongue.

RAY *exits, clanging the door shut.* LIZZIE *sings a lullaby.*

LIZZIE:

Hushabye, you naughty girl
Don't you make another peep.
No one worse in the world
Time to go to sleep.

The second verse is interrupted by RAY *banging on the bars.*

RAY: [*off*] Quiet in there!

LIZZIE:

God has seen the things you do,

How you make your parents weep –
RAY: [*off*] Be quiet, or I'll switch the light off.
LIZZIE:

There'll be no place in Heaven for you.
Time to go to sleep.

Darkness. She continues to the end of the song.

No one knows you, no one cares.
You're not in your mother's prayers.
All you know to do is lie
Hush, hushabye.

In the darkness the Wolf appears and tries to swallow LIZZIE.
She cries out. A harsh light is switched on. ANGELA *addresses*
RAY, *pulling off* LIZZIE's *wet underpants and wrapping them
in a plastic bag.*

ANGELA: What were you *thinking*?
RAY: You weren't home.
ANGELA: But what – ? You can't *do* that! You can't take a child out of
school – without permission –
RAY: We tried to contact you, Mrs Gael.
ANGELA: I go to pick her up, and she's not there. All the other kids
come out. How do you think I felt?
RAY: I –
ANGELA: So I go to the office, in a panic, and they say she's at the
police station! Jesus!
RAY: Theft is a police matter. The school gave full permission.
ANGELA: I'm her mother. It's not up to them!
RAY: I trust the teacher sent a note home yesterday, about the birds.
ANGELA: If it's up to anyone to deal with her, it's me.
RAY: You weren't home. We tried to contact you.
ANGELA: Me or her father.
RAY: You were at work.
ANGELA: Understand?
RAY: Most single mothers have trouble with discipline. They're grateful
for our help.
ANGELA: Just – please – never do that again.
RAY: That's up to her. I hope we won't need to.

ANGELA: And the light – ? She has bad enough nightmares already, Sergeant. She hardly sleeps as it is.

RAY: Well let's hope for all our sakes that's the last of it. [*To* LIZZIE] You think you can keep out of trouble from now on?

LIZZIE: The Wolf came.

ANGELA: [*to* RAY] Tomorrow's Christmas Eve!

RAY: Look. She's not the first. I've done it to others and I can assure you, they don't need psychotherapy after. On the contrary: they never set a foot wrong again.

LIZZIE: The Wolf came back, Mum.

RAY: I keep an eye on them through the peep-hole. And it's never for more than half an hour.

ANGELA: She's nine years old!

LIZZIE: The Wolf.

RAY: Just to teach them a lesson.

LIZZIE: Mummy.

RAY: If the mothers are out working ...

ANGELA: Yes! It's criminal, isn't it?!

SCENE FOUR

The house. WARREN *has a Christmas present for* LIZZIE. ANGELA *laughs as:*

WARREN: [*singing*]
'Joy to the world,
Your Dad has come,
So how about a beer?'

ANGELA *gives him a beer.* LIZZIE *looks at* WARREN*'s present.*

ANGELA: [*to* LIZZIE] Well? Go on!

WARREN: She's awestruck, aren't you, Liz? How about a hello?

LIZZIE: Hello, Dad.

ANGELA: Let's see what it is!

LIZZIE: I don't want any presents.

WARREN: Now that's what I call a Christmas miracle.

ANGELA: [*to* LIZZIE] What are you talking about? [*To* WARREN] She's been asking what you'll bring her since *last* Christmas. [*To* LIZZIE] Of course you do! And you've got something for Dad, haven't you?

LIZZIE *runs out.*

Do I get anything?

WARREN: Last month's school fees. Sorry it's late.

ANGELA: Gee. You shouldn't have.

WARREN: Plus I'm taking you out to tea.

ANGELA: Listen: a couple of days ago Lizzie got in trouble.

WARREN: What happened?

ANGELA: Just shoplifting. She was pretty upset. Yesterday she disappeared 'til dinnertime –

LIZZIE *runs back in and gives* WARREN *a page.*

WARREN: What's this?

LIZZIE: I wrote you a poem.

ANGELA: No, remember we went shopping? What you bought Dad?

WARREN: Your writing's getting neater.

ANGELA: The real present ...

WARREN: But your spelling's a worry. Don't give up your day job, kiddo.

ANGELA: Remember ... ?

Beat.

From the mall.

Beat.

In silver paper.

LIZZIE *bursts into tears.*

LIZZIE: I ate them!

She hurls herself sobbing to the floor.

WARREN: I just hope they weren't drill bits, that's all.

ANGELA: Lizzie ...

WARREN: Or socks.

LIZZIE: They were chocolates! And I ate them!

ANGELA *laughs uncomfortably.*

ANGELA: I told you they'd be safer in my room. Come on ...

LIZZIE: I'm sorry. I'm so, so sorry!

WARREN: Hey, you just spared me a faceful of zits.

ANGELA: Lizzie, it doesn't matter. It's alright.

LIZZIE: I opened them and ate all of them. I'm bad, I'm bad.

WARREN: I've still got my poem.

   LIZZIE *tears it to pieces.*

LIZZIE: It's stupid! I hate it!

ANGELA: What is wrong?

WARREN: Come here, open your present.

LIZZIE: Don't give me presents. I'm too naughty. Oh, I love you! I love you!

ANGELA: You're not naughty.

LIZZIE: Yesterday I was.

ANGELA: Everyone makes mistakes.

LIZZIE: But yesterday I was!

ANGELA: Yesterday?

WARREN: Come here.

LIZZIE: You shouldn't have had me. You should've got a good girl. Because you're the best ones in the world.

ANGELA: That's enough of that.

LIZZIE: You can smack me if you want.

WARREN: [*laughing*] When do I ever smack you?

LIZZIE: I'll buy you some more.

ANGELA: That's a good idea. Dad can take you on Saturday. I think you should open your present.

WARREN: I'd never smack you, Lizzie.

LIZZIE: I promise to be good. Forever and ever. I never want to make you angry.

ANGELA: Darling. Nothing you do can make us cross. You're our little girl. Now stop being silly and open it.

LIZZIE: No, no.

WARREN: That's a rude thing to do, say no when someone gives you a present. If you don't want me to be angry – if you want to make me happy, open it.

ANGELA: Lizzie. Is it about that policeman?

WARREN: Did he scare you?

LIZZIE: No.

Pause.

Yes.

WARREN: Stupid clown. He'll hear from me.

ANGELA: [*to* LIZZIE] It's all in the past now. All gone.

LIZZIE: I'll buy you some more, Dad. Gran sent me five dollars.

WARREN: All I want for Christmas is you to open your present.

She opens it. It's a big doll. WARREN *kisses her.*

Happy Christmas, darling.

SCENE FIVE

Wasteland. LIZZIE *is motionless on the ground, one arm askew, eyes staring.* RAY *stands looking down at her for a few moments. Then he takes out a notebook and jots notes as he speaks.*

RAY: Righto.

LIZZIE *doesn't move.*

Thanks love ...

LIZZIE: See, one arm was funny ... like this.

RAY: You can get up now.

LIZZIE: This was the spot.

LIZZIE *gets up carefully, almost reverently.*

RAY: We know.

LIZZIE: He had one hand all black, and dirt on his face. And he had stuff on his mouth. Like fluff.

RAY: Slaver. You didn't touch him, did you?

LIZZIE *nods.*

You shouldn't have done that.

LIZZIE: We didn't know if he was dead for sure.

RAY: You didn't move him?

LIZZIE: No, I just touched his mouth. Because it was blue.

RAY: But you didn't shift him, did you? Into another position? He was just like he was when the workmen found him today?

LIZZIE: Blue and cold. And he had little flowers and grass all over him.

RAY: So that's how he was lying? Just like you showed me?

LIZZIE *nods.*

And there was nothing else around? No – ... You kids didn't pinch anything? Take anything?

LIZZIE *shakes her head.*

LIZZIE: Do you know who it was yet?

RAY: Not yet. You'd better get yourself home.

LIZZIE: What'll you do to them when you get them?

RAY: Something nasty, don't you worry.

LIZZIE: What?

RAY: I don't want to give you bad dreams. Come on, love.

LIZZIE: What did the baby's mum do? Did she cry?

RAY: Yes.

LIZZIE: I already get bad dreams. Tell me what you'll do.

RAY: It's getting dark. Home you go.

LIZZIE: Will she miss her baby?

RAY: 'Course she will.

LIZZIE: Who do you think did it?

RAY: You do what your mum says, you don't wag school, you stick with your mates, and there'll be nothing for you to worry about. You certainly won't be playing here any more.

LIZZIE: I'm not scared of anything.

Beat.

RAY: Elizabeth. Why didn't you tell?

LIZZIE: Tell what?

RAY: You kids knew he was here for two days. This is where you play, isn't it?

LIZZIE *nods.*

He went missing Christmas Eve. You lot found him that afternoon. The workmen found him this morning. That's two days. Why didn't you tell anyone?

LIZZIE: Well we didn't know he was dead for sure.

RAY: He didn't get up and play with you, did he?
LIZZIE: No sir.
RAY: Now Lizzie, I think you told a lie. Shall I tell you why?
LIZZIE: No.
RAY: Because I asked if you kids touched anything, and you said 'No'.
But I can see these blocks have been moved. To hide him.
LIZZIE: No sir.
RAY: Don't tell me 'No'. I can see very well that they used to be there.
There's no grass; look at all the slaters.
LIZZIE: I never lied, sir.
RAY: Now you're lying again.
LIZZIE: No, you said, did we touch the baby? We never moved him.
We just moved the concrete things.

RAY *realises she's right.*

RAY: Well what did you do that for?

Silence.

Well?
LIZZIE: It wasn't for grown-ups.
RAY: What?
LIZZIE: It was a secret.
RAY: I don't understand.
LIZZIE: You have things you don't tell us. We wanted our own secret.
RAY: Who ... ? You and your three mates?
LIZZIE: First.
RAY: And then?
LIZZIE: More.
RAY: How many more?
LIZZIE: Kids at school.
RAY: Half? All?

LIZZIE *nods.*

All? Looks like we've got a lot of interviewing to do.
LIZZIE: I felt sorry for his mum.
RAY: Thanks for your help, Lizzie.
LIZZIE: I wanted to be good.
RAY: You've been very good. Very helpful. Thank you. You go home
now.

Anthony Phelan as Ray in the 1996 Griffin Theatre production. Photo Robert McFarlane.

LIZZIE: Sir? Can I see Toby?

RAY: No love. Toby's dead.

LIZZIE: Oh I know that. I mean can I see him in his little coffin?

Beat.

RAY: Are you a good reader, Lizzie?

LIZZIE: Yep. Sir.

RAY: Big words too?

LIZZIE: All words.

RAY: I wonder if you can show me how clever you are. [*Indicating the graffiti*] I wonder if you can read those words for me.

LIZZIE: No. I can't read that.

RAY: Why? Is it too hard?

LIZZIE: No.

RAY: Too messy?

LIZZIE: It's not messy.

RAY: Does it upset you, then? To read it?

LIZZIE: No. It's just someone having fun.

RAY: 'I murder so that I may come back'. Is that funny?

LIZZIE shrugs.

Why would someone play a prank like that?

LIZZIE: I don't know!

RAY: Morbid, isn't it?

LIZZIE: Something to do!

RAY: Vandalism's a criminal offence.

LIZZIE runs off. RAY is alone with the invisible corpse. He speaks into a tape recorder.

Subject: Toby Brian Chester. Age at time of death: two and a half years. This report recorded two days after subject's death. Circumstances suspicious. Subject discovered by railway workers, apparently hidden with intent behind concrete blocks, in the vacant lot by the tracks. Attempt at concealment indicated: subject covered with handfuls of weeds. Subject's body in state of preliminary decomposition. Scratches on arms and face indicate a struggle. Small bite marks and bruises on legs. Some bleeding. No sexual interference. Double punctures in throat, like dog's teeth. Fangs.

Inflicted with scissors. Cause of death at first not apparent. On more detailed examination, appears to be death by strangulation. The fingermarks on the throat are small, the pressure featherlight ...

He examines closely, and is shocked by his realisation.

I think we're looking for a child.

CHILDREN: [*off*]

> Old Granny Gray,
> She let me out to play;
> I can't go near the wa-ter
> To hunt the ducks away.
> Over the garden wall
> I let the baby fall.
> Me mother come out
> And give me a clout
> And knocked me over
> A bottle of stout.

SCENE SIX

Police station. WARREN, ANGELA, LIZZIE, RAY.

RAY: [*to the parents*] You shouldn't have brought her. This is a private interview.

ANGELA: You wanted both of us.

WARREN: You pay for a baby-sitter, mate.

RAY: [*to* LIZZIE] Righto, you. Think you can be quiet over there for ten minutes? [*to* WARREN] Simple questions, just answer 'Yes' or 'No'.

ANGELA: I live with her.

WARREN: Yeah, ask Ange.

RAY: Please yourselves.

LIZZIE: Can I have some paper to draw on?

RAY: I asked *you* to be quiet.

WARREN: Give her the back of something.

RAY, long-suffering, finds scrap paper.

RAY: Just to reassure you, Mr and Mrs Gael, this is normal police procedure. There's nothing to worry about. We're talking to all the parents. It's how we eliminate your child from the picture. Alright?

LIZZIE: Can I have some pencils?

RAY *finds the textas he confiscated, and after a moment's dilemma, hands them to her.*

RAY: [*under his breath*] Dear little thing.

WARREN: Fire away.

RAY: 'Do any of these words describe your child?' A 'Yes' or 'No''ll do. 'Sly'. 'Insolent'. 'Bullying'. 'Eager to please' –

ANGELA: Wait. What?

RAY: 'Sly'. 'Insolent' –

ANGELA: She's not 'sly'. That's an awful word.

WARREN: Yeah, what is this? A *form*?

RAY: Well say 'No'. I'm putting the kettle on here.

ANGELA: How does this help?

RAY: Investigation.

WARREN: Some *form*? To find a killer? What is it, who wrote it?

RAY: It's standard procedure. A psychiatrist. I dunno. This is what they give us. [*Indicating the coffee*] I've only got instant.

WARREN: A kid ...

ANGELA: But those words –

RAY: I'll take that as 'No' then.

ANGELA: 'Sly', 'insolent' –

WARREN: Psychos are violent. Not kids.

RAY: 'Rejects authority'. 'Yes'.

ANGELA: Who doesn't?

WARREN: What'll it prove?

RAY: They'll put together a character study, and then go through these files. It's very simple, just a one-word answer. 'Easily tempted to pilfer'.

ANGELA: No.

RAY: Coles.

WARREN: Once!

ANGELA: Twice.

RAY: Don't give yourself a headache over it. 'Disruptive in class'. 'Influenced by others' –

WARREN: No. No.

RAY: 'Plays truant'. 'Yes'.

ANGELA: All kids do. That doesn't mean anything.

RAY: None of it means anything. We just have to file a form. 'Popular with other children'.

WARREN: Yes. That's a 'yes'.

ANGELA: Except those notes from the teacher.

WARREN: What notes?

ANGELA: Being rough.

WARREN: *Lizzie?* When?

RAY: Please. I've got sixteen more of these to get through tonight.

ANGELA: And what do the other parents say?

RAY: They say they can't understand it.

WARREN: *No-one* can / understand it.

RAY: They can't believe their child knew and didn't say anything. For two days. I can't.

ANGELA: Lizzie was the one who spoke up. Surely, if all this tells you anything –

RAY: It's a good sign. Yes.

WARREN: Yeah, there's nowhere to write *that*, is there?

ANGELA: I won't just say 'bullying', 'sly'. It feels wrong.

RAY: Then say 'No'.

ANGELA: No, I mean –

WARREN: I hope you're not just doing kids. There's plenty of weirdos out there.

RAY: We're doing our job. 'Answers back in class'.

ANGELA: This is ridiculous!

RAY: What do you suggest then, Mrs Gael? – I presume that's still your name?

ANGELA: I suggest you look at the things that count. What kind of homes they come from. What they watch on TV.

RAY: Frankly I think that's all garbage. The simple fact is: some kids are born evil.

WARREN: What ... like genes?

RAY: Some kids are bad eggs. I don't call myself a scientist.

LIZZIE *tries to show* WARREN *her drawing.*

LIZZIE: Dad.

WARREN: [*to* RAY] You mean like they're marked? From birth?

RAY: They've done tests on brains and that. If you could see the brain before the kid was born, you could terminate it, and save everyone a lot of trouble.

LIZZIE: Do you want to see my drawing?

WARREN: So some people are just born like that. Can't help themselves.

ANGELA: I don't like that idea.

RAY: I dare say. But what can you do? It's out of our control. Can we finish?

LIZZIE: Dad?

WARREN: [*to the adults*] I reckon it's genes. That makes sense. Dad's a long-jumper, kid's a long-jumper.

ANGELA: What do you mean, 'born evil'? How can that happen?

RAY: Freaks of nature. Look at Hitler: nothing wrong with his home life. Yet you get all your experts, lying him on the couch and putting his crimes down to 'Dad didn't love me', 'Mum was a lush'. Most children are good as little lambs. But once in a while, a monster's born.

ANGELA: What parent is going to swallow that?

WARREN: Genes are scientific.

RAY: I meet 'em all the time. In my line of work. Juvenile offenders. You only have to look at their eyes.

LIZZIE *tries to show* ANGELA *the drawing.*

LIZZIE: Mum?

ANGELA: [*to* RAY] And what do you see?

RAY: I don't know! Evil! [*Indicating the questionnaire*] That'll do. Sign the bottom of the form.

WARREN *signs.*

WARREN: Righto then. Want a lift home, love?

LIZZIE: I drew something for show-and-tell.

ANGELA: [*to* RAY, *signing*] No one with a child could believe that.

RAY: Look, it should come as a relief to you. I don't know what you're worried about. I've got kids. You and I managed to slip through untouched. Most parents do. It's just the few unfortunates.

ANGELA: Like Mrs Hitler.

WARREN: [*to* ANGELA] You ever killed anyone?

ANGELA: No.

WARREN: There you go. The point is, love, we don't have to worry. Some poor bugger does, but not us. Sure I can't drop you?

> ANGELA *shakes her head.* LIZZIE *holds up the drawing.*

LIZZIE: Dad?

WARREN: Beautiful. See you Saturday, Liz.

> *He exits.*

ANGELA: Didn't you ever feel like you could do something ... bad? When you were a kid?

> *Beat.*

RAY: No. No, I didn't. Always knew I wanted to be a cop.

> *An awkward silence.*

Why? Did you?

ANGELA: No.

> ANGELA *stands.*

Give back the textas, Lizzie.

> RAY *counts them. She shows him the drawing.*

RAY: Very nice. What's it meant to be?

ANGELA: Let's not take up any more of the Sergeant's time. Put your stuff in the bin, darling, and we can go home.

LIZZIE: The Wolf.

RAY: Looks more like a horse. You've got to learn to draw fur. Start off with dogs.

LIZZIE: It's frightening.

> RAY *mugs fear.* ANGELA *laughs, screwing up the drawing.*

ANGELA: Don't encourage her.

> RAY *takes the drawing to throw away as* ANGELA *and* LIZZIE *exit.*

SCENE SEVEN

Wasteland. ANGELA *stands by the site of the death. In one hand she holds Lizzie's school shoes; in the other, a white lily. She kneels and places the flower on the site. She is uneasy, and her discomfort grows as she sees the graffiti. Enter* WARREN.

WARREN: I came.

> *Silence.*

Angie?

ANGELA: Have you seen it?

WARREN: I didn't intend to.

ANGELA: Such a small space. All these flowers ...

WARREN: Cards, teddy bears ... at a murder site. Gives me the creeps.

ANGELA: And his mother ...

WARREN: Don't think about it, love. Why'd you call me? To this place?

> ANGELA *shrugs.*

I get this urgent message. I'm on my shift, Ange.

> *Pause.*

You alright?

ANGELA: You were supposed to pick her up yesterday.

WARREN: Yeah, I rang the school. Terry wanted to swap shifts. She got home okay, didn't she?

ANGELA: But I was at work. She was locked out.

WARREN: Shit. Sorry.

ANGELA: I got home at six and she was on the doorstep.

WARREN: Why didn't she go to the salon?

ANGELA: Because I gave her a big talk about not walking around alone ... after what happened. And so she didn't. She sat on the doorstep for two hours.

WARREN: You've got to give her a key.

ANGELA: But that's the point, Warren! I don't want her coming home alone! She's nine years old!

WARREN: I made a mistake.

ANGELA: Didn't you *think*? It's Wednesday. I work.

WARREN: I'm really sorry. Really.

ANGELA: It was nearly dark!

WARREN *laughs.*

WARREN: Is that all? Couldn't it wait till Saturday?

ANGELA: I don't know what to do any more.

WARREN: Come on, Missus, I'll drive you home.

ANGELA: What if I did that? Decided to drop everything so I could go to a piss-up? Then / what would happen to Lizzie?

WARREN: Who says it was a piss-up?

ANGELA: It's alright for you. It's just a quick phone call if you decide to vanish for the weekend. If you bother to remember *that*. But *I* can't just run away!

WARREN: Why is there suddenly a problem? You wanted it like this. With Lizzie.

ANGELA: Yeah, well it's getting to me. Where do you go, anyway? All your drives?

WARREN: Hate giving back the cab with petrol still in it. He rips me off enough as it is. To the foot-hills. Burnie, for a pub breakfast. Nowhere special.

ANGELA: Why?

WARREN: Because I can't breathe here. This town. It's like being stuck in a lift.

ANGELA: And then what? When you move to the mainland? What'll I do then? When'll she see you?

WARREN: It's not going to happen for ages. Don't think about it.

ANGELA: I hate this place too! I can't bear it! But I'm stuck here – because I've got a kid!

WARREN: That's why I'm still here. She's my kid too.

ANGELA: Well I wish you weren't! I wish you'd go! And take Lizzie with you! Take her, take her away.

She bursts into tears and beats WARREN *with the shoes.*

WARREN: Angie! For Christ's sake –

ANGELA: Just go away! I can't stand to look at you! You make me sick!

He grabs her wrists, the shoes fall. She collapses.

WARREN: What the hell's got into you?

ANGELA: There's blood on them.

WARREN: What?

ANGELA: Spots of blood. Look.

> WARREN *laughs.*

What'll we do?

WARREN: About what? What do you mean?

ANGELA: We'll have to tell.

WARREN: This is what you're all worked up about? Lizzie's shoes?

ANGELA: We'll have to take her in.

WARREN: Stop it.

ANGELA: They were on the kitchen table. She's always so neat, she never ... I picked them up. I saw brown spots.

> WARREN *holds her.*

WARREN: [*gently*] Ange. You're going mad.

> ANGELA *cannot speak.*

That's the most insane thing I've ever heard you say. I don't know you like this.

ANGELA: Is it blood? Not paint?

WARREN: I don't want you to say any more.

ANGELA: You have to look at them.

WARREN: No. I'm not going to. Because you're being silly. You're not funny. You're being stupid. I'm taking you home.

ANGELA: Just look at them.

> WARREN *grabs the shoes, looks, and flings them back.*

WARREN: It's mud. It's nothing. She cut herself. She's always falling over.

ANGELA: That's her writing. I swear it. I know it.

WARREN: So what?

ANGELA: What'll we do? What'll we do? Take her in? And they lock her up? Put her on trial in a court? And that will be *it*. She's had no life yet!

WARREN: Just stop it.

ANGELA: Or we don't tell. We just go on as normal. But every time we look at her, we'll know!

WARREN: Stop.

ANGELA: She did it.

WARREN: Christ, Angela!

ANGELA: I know.

WARREN: What do you know? How?

ANGELA: *I just know!*

> *Silence.*

We've got to decide what to do. You have to think with me.

WARREN: You keep your madwoman thoughts to yourself. I don't want any part of it. I'm on my shift.

ANGELA: Warren! You can't just go every time you don't want to hear something!

WARREN: I'm not listening to lies – evil – about my daughter.

ANGELA: Help me!

WARREN: Can you hear yourself?! Do you know what you're saying? It's like you're possessed. That's *Lizzie* you're talking about. You've flipped, Angela. Go and get something from the chemist. I'm not talking to you like this. You frighten me.

ANGELA: I'm frightened.

WARREN: I can't believe we're even having this conversation. We're going to be laughing about it next week.

ANGELA: I don't know what to do.

WARREN: Then I'll tell you. Go home, have a stiff drink, and watch a funny video. Wake up, for Christ's sake.

ANGELA: I am awake.

WARREN: Angie, please. Stop this.

ANGELA: You know it too.

WARREN: No ...

ANGELA: Don't you?

WARREN: Just stop.

ANGELA: Warren?

WARREN: No.

ANGELA: There's no going back.

WARREN: Christ Almighty! There's nothing to find out.

ANGELA: Just pretend. Just imagine there is. Then what?

WARREN: I'll go mad.

ANGELA: I'll go mad if we never know.

WARREN: Why has it got to be your word over mine?

ANGELA: You wanted me to look after her. You *told* me to make the decisions.

WARREN: That'd be the end of her.

ANGELA: I know. What's wrong with me?

Silence. ANGELA *goes to touch* WARREN, *but he turns away.*

WARREN: I'm late.

ANGELA: Warren. Help me.

He starts to exit.

If you care, if you're my friend, if you love Lizzie – help me!

He exits.

SCENE EIGHT

LIZZIE's *world.* LIZZIE *and the Wolf.*

CHILDREN: [*off*]

There is a little girl, 'Lizzie' is her name.
She has a pet Wolf who is good and tame.
They play like friends, it's just a game,
But sometimes he goes mad.

And then the little Wolf turns big and black.
Up stands every hair on his back.
His eyes go red and he'll attack
And he'll do something bad.

He pounces on Lizzie with a mighty roar.
He opens up his jaws like a big trap-door.
And then she can see the light no more,
Sliding down his throat.

[*Whispering*]
  The stomach of the Wolf is a big black pit,
  And down she goes till she falls in it.
  It's dark and hot and it's full of shit,
  She cannot stay afloat.

  Lizzie thrashes all about,
  She cannot see and she cannot shout,
  She cannot breathe and she can't get out.
  Lizzie! Lizzie! *Lizzie!*

SCENE NINE

LIZZIE's *bedroom, night. The low rumbling of the Wolf. The room begins to shake. The rumbling increases.* LIZZIE *puts her hands over her ears.*

LIZZIE: Make it stop. I want my mum. Go away.

  She cowers.

  Trouble. Trouble!

  The Wolf is enveloping her. She screams. ANGELA *appears, holds her.*

ANGELA: Who are you talking to?

LIZZIE: The Wolf.

ANGELA: There's no wolves here. Shhh. Little girls have nothing to be scared of.

LIZZIE: He was here. He gets in.

ANGELA: No he doesn't.

LIZZIE: But I saw him.

ANGELA: I told you not to read stories. They're all pretend.

LIZZIE: Lies?

ANGELA: Yes.

LIZZIE: Stories are lies ...

ANGELA: I don't like you making things up.

LIZZIE: Playing is made up.

ANGELA: Nice things either. You'll only be disappointed.

She hugs LIZZIE.

So no more silliness.

LIZZIE: Mum.

ANGELA: Yes?

LIZZIE: Do you ever think bad things?

ANGELA: What do you mean?

LIZZIE: Horrible things that won't go away.

ANGELA: Of course not.

LIZZIE: Because you're good?

ANGELA: No, because no one does. Especially little girls. Only big people
worry. You've got nothing to do but be the angel you are. [*Hugging
her*] Now, did you see anything, or not?

LIZZIE: No.

ANGELA: Nothing at all? No wolf?

LIZZIE: No, Mum.

ANGELA: You're too good to tell stories, aren't you Lizzie?

LIZZIE: Yes.

ANGELA: You would never lie to me.

LIZZIE: No.

ANGELA: I want you to tell me something. Will you tell the truth?

LIZZIE: Yes.

ANGELA: What are the spots on your school shoes?

Silence.

What are they, Lizzie? Tell me. You won't get in trouble.

LIZZIE: I cut my finger.

ANGELA: Blood ... ? Show me where.

LIZZIE: It's better now.

ANGELA: That's not the truth, is it? If you want to make Mummy happy,
tell the truth.

Pause.

Where's it from?

LIZZIE: [*whispering*] I don't know.

ANGELA: Lizzie. Is it from the baby?

LIZZIE: No.

ANGELA: I think it might be.

LIZZIE: No, it isn't.

ANGELA: I'm going to give you one hour to think about it. I'm going to lock your door. And when I come back, we'll see if you remember the truth.

LIZZIE: Don't lock the door.

ANGELA: And I'm going to take the light.

LIZZIE: No.

ANGELA: And just see what you remember.

LIZZIE: [as ANGELA *goes to take the night-light*] No, Mum! He'll come back!

ANGELA: There's no such thing as wolves.

Pause.

He only comes for little girls who tell lies.

She takes the light.

LIZZIE: No, Mum! Please don't!

ANGELA: He does horrible things to liars. Horrible things.

ANGELA *goes to close the door.*

We'll see in an hour.

LIZZIE: No, Mum! I remember! I remember!

ANGELA: What?

LIZZIE: He done it. I was there.

ANGELA: Who?

LIZZIE: He cut it. With stones.

ANGELA: Who did?

LIZZIE: Don't take the light.

ANGELA: Were you playing at the weeds when the baby died?

LIZZIE: Yes.

ANGELA: Were you alone when he died?

LIZZIE: No.

ANGELA: Were you?

LIZZIE *is silent.* ANGELA *makes to leave again with the light.*

LIZZIE: Yes!

ANGELA: Did you make him die, Lizzie?

LIZZIE: No Mum! Don't take the light!
ANGELA: Lizzie ... ?
LIZZIE: No!
ANGELA: 'No' or 'Yes'?
LIZZIE: He'll get me!
ANGELA: So that means you're telling stories? You're a liar?
LIZZIE: No!
ANGELA: Did you make him die? All I want is the truth!
LIZZIE: No.
ANGELA: Did you or didn't you?!
LIZZIE: No.
ANGELA: I'll ask you one more time. One more time, then I leave you
    to the wolf. Did you or didn't you?
LIZZIE: No!

> ANGELA *exits and locks the door, leaving the room in*
> *darkness.*

Yes! Yes! Come back, Mum!

> *The light comes on. A long moment. Then* ANGELA *pulls* LIZZIE
> *out of bed, and puts her in her dressing gown.*

Where are we going?
ANGELA: To see Sergeant Ray.
LIZZIE: Why?
ANGELA: I want you to tell him about Saturday.
LIZZIE: What about Saturday?
ANGELA: Jesus Christ, Jesus ...
LIZZIE: Am I in trouble?

> ANGELA *laughs and cries.*

I never took the baby, Mum.

> ANGELA *brushes* LIZZIE's *hair.*

ANGELA: Keep still.
LIZZIE: Are they going to hang me?
ANGELA: No.
LIZZIE: What'll they do to me?
ANGELA: Nothing. Nothing.

LIZZIE: I never, Mum.

ANGELA: They'll take your fingerprints. Test that blood.

LIZZIE: I never touched him, Mum.

>   ANGELA *pulls* LIZZIE*'s shoes on.*

ANGELA: Just tell them the truth.

LIZZIE: If you touch someone, do your fingerprints stay on their skin?

>   ANGELA, *overcome, ties* LIZZIE*'s shoes.*

> If you drag someone really hard, do your nails stay in them?

>   ANGELA *does up* LIZZIE*'s buttons.*

> Does their skin come off on you? Does it? Mum? Does it?

SCENE TEN

Police station. LIZZIE *is in her dressing gown with her doll.* ANGELA *sits nearby. The school shoes are on the desk.*

RAY: Now I'm going to be recording this. I want you to say 'Yes' or 'No'. Don't nod your head, because we can't hear that. Alright?

>   LIZZIE *nods. When* RAY *goes to reprimand her, she giggles.*

LIZZIE: Yes sir.

RAY: And I must tell you that anything you say can be used in evidence against you. Do you understand what that means?

LIZZIE: Yeah.

ANGELA: She doesn't.

LIZZIE: No.

RAY: It means you've got to tell the truth. Or you'll be in big trouble. Alright?

LIZZIE: Alright.

RAY: Elizabeth, when did you last see Toby Chester?

LIZZIE: At the weeds.

RAY: You mean the vacant lot. Near the train tracks.

LIZZIE: Yes, sir.

RAY: On Saturday. The day he died.

LIZZIE: No, sir.

RAY: You just said –

LIZZIE: [*sing-song*]

> Where'd you catch your cold, sir?
> From the North Pole, sir.
> What / were you doing there, sir?

ANGELA: Lizzie.

LIZZIE: [*to Ray*] Yes.

RAY: So you were there in the morning, playing in the same spot where later that day he was killed.

> LIZZIE *nods.*

Speak up.

LIZZIE: Yes!

RAY: Even though when I talked to all the children, you said you weren't.

ANGELA: Answer the question! If you said 'No' before and 'Yes' now, then you've been telling stories!

RAY: Don't get angry. [*To* LIZZIE] You were there on Saturday morning?

LIZZIE: Playing with my friends.

RAY: And how did you get blood on your shoes?

LIZZIE: Maybe ...

RAY: I beg your pardon?

LIZZIE: 'Mrs Arden there's a chicken in your garden'.

ANGELA: Do you want a smack?

LIZZIE: Maybe when we were fighting.

RAY: You and who?

LIZZIE: Errol and Norman and Tracy and them.

RAY: And Toby?

LIZZIE: No, he's too young.

RAY: But he was there.

LIZZIE: Yes, sir.

> ANGELA *turns away.*

RAY: And in the fighting, someone got hurt and started bleeding.

LIZZIE: Or maybe it was my nose-bleed.

ANGELA: She doesn't get nose-bleeds.

RAY: Is that right? You don't?

> LIZZIE *shakes her head.*

'Yes' or 'No', Lizzie. We can't hear that.

LIZZIE: [*whispering*] No.

RAY: Did anyone else have blood on them?

LIZZIE: No.

RAY: No. And was Toby okay?

LIZZIE: What?

RAY: Was Toby alright?

LIZZIE: No. He's dead.

RAY: When you last saw him?

LIZZIE: Yeah.

RAY: So after you finished playing, whose responsibility was it to take him home?

LIZZIE: What?

ANGELA: I beg your pardon, sir.

RAY: Who ... Whose job was it to make sure he got home alright? You live the closest, don't you?

LIZZIE: No.

ANGELA: Yes we do.

LIZZIE: Yes.

RAY: So I think it was probably your job.

LIZZIE: I could never hurt a fly. I couldn't strangle a baby. That's horrible, that.

> *Beat.*

RAY: How'd you know he was strangled, Lizzie?

LIZZIE: I want to go home now.

RAY: Sit down, love. We're not through yet.

LIZZIE: This is brainwashing. I'll get some solicitors.

ANGELA: Lizzie!

LIZZIE: Is this place bugged?

ANGELA: Behave yourself!

LIZZIE: He's saying I killed the baby, Mum.

RAY: No, I'm only trying to establish –

LIZZIE: I never took the baby! I never touched it! Youse are trying to say I did it, but I never! I never!

ANGELA: Sit up straight.

LIZZIE: I don't know why. It was last week. I keep forgetting.

RAY: Forgetting what?

> LIZZIE *is silent.*

> Lizzie. Do you want all this to be over?

> *She nods.*

> So do I. I'm not dragging it on just to spite *you*. Alright?

> *She nods.*

> I need to know what happened. Then we can all go back to normal.

> *Beat.*

LIZZIE: We were playing chasings and I hid behind the blocks and I tripped over something. I looked down and it was Toby's head.

> *Pause.*

> I go, 'Who did this?' and out jumps the Moron.

RAY: Who?

LIZZIE: He's a slow boy in our class. We call him the Moron, but his real name's Andy.

> RAY *looks to* ANGELA.

ANGELA: Andy Ruttledge.

LIZZIE: Andy Ruttledge, yes. Anyway, he's grinning all over and he goes, 'Me! I done that! I strangled him then I made them little holes!' and we all go, 'You never', and so he goes, 'Look!'

RAY: What?

LIZZIE: Scissors. They were silver scissors with black handles. And something wrong with them, like one leg was bent. We still go, 'No, you never', so he passed them around and we all had a look. And then we knew he did.

RAY: How?

LIZZIE: There was blood on them.

RAY: Oh ... And you say he had them behind his back?

LIZZIE: No. Before, in the morning, he hid the scissors in the grass. He rustled around like this and found them. And I know they were his, because I saw him playing with them at school. And once I saw him try to cut off a cat's tail.

RAY: [*to* ANGELA] Do you know this boy?

ANGELA: Yes.

LIZZIE: He's a wild one, isn't he Mum? Our teacher's always going, 'That Andy Ruttledge ...'

ANGELA: [*to* RAY] He's simple.

RAY *goes through his files.*

LIZZIE: And I seen him before, picking on Toby. He can't stand up to the big boys, so he picks on the little ones. I seen him smacking Toby once.

ANGELA: Why we didn't think of him ...

LIZZIE: And he's slow. So maybe he didn't know he was hurting him.

ANGELA: You tripped. In these shoes.

LIZZIE: Maybe he thought it was funny, 'cause he was laughing and laughing, going 'Ha ha ha ha!' When he was smacking him, and when he showed us them scissors.

RAY *reads a file.*

RAY: It all sounds highly probable. Except for the fact that he was at the airport that day.

LIZZIE: No he wasn't.

RAY: 'Andrew Ruttledge, interviewed separately and with his parents, was seeing off his godmother at Launceston airport. The flight was at four, so they drove down early and made a day of it. Verified by Ansett staff and a petrol station attendant.' That was the day Toby died.

LIZZIE: Then he's lying.

RAY: Somebody's lying. But you've given us a very detailed description of those scissors. And they haven't been mentioned in the papers.

LIZZIE: I don't want to play this any more.

ANGELA *goes to a window.* LIZZIE *watches her as she answers* RAY.

RAY: You're a slippery customer, aren't you?

LIZZIE: No.

RAY: That's a very wicked thing to do, blame someone else. Especially a slow boy.

LIZZIE: But I thought it was him. It might've been, Mum ...

RAY: I want the truth now. No more mucking around. The truth.

LIZZIE *hugs the doll.*

*Lucy Bell as Lizzie and Tara Morice as Angela in the 1996 Griffin
Theatre production. Photo Robert McFarlane.*

LIZZIE: I want Dad.

RAY: Lizzie. Show us your dolly, will you?

ANGELA *swipes it from her.*

Now I'm going to sit her up here, on this chair, and I want you to show me what you were playing with Toby.

LIZZIE: When the others went?

Beat.

RAY: Yes. When they went home.

LIZZIE: It was just a game.

RAY: Show me.

LIZZIE: Just dumb. Something to do.

RAY: I'd like to see.

LIZZIE: You can't get in trouble for games, can you?

RAY *nods for her to stand.* LIZZIE *walks around the doll.*

I showed him this. It's only my bus pass.

RAY *nods.* LIZZIE *addresses the doll.*

Okay, then. I am the police and who's been breaking school windows? Don't give me that smiling. I think it was you. I think you're telling stories, young man. I think we better teach you a lesson.

LIZZIE *picks up the doll, then turns to* RAY *for approval.*

SCENE ELEVEN

Wasteland. LIZZIE *has run away. She is setting up a place to sleep amongst the weeds. She hears whimpering.*

LIZZIE: Baby ...

Her eyes follow a figure only visible to her.

Go home, baby. This is my place.

TOBY: [*off*] I want me mum.

LIZZIE: Well she's not here.

TOBY: [*off*] I don't like it here.

LIZZIE: Get lost, then.

TOBY: [*off, crying*] I want me mum!

LIZZIE: [*mimicking*] 'I want me mum!'

TOBY: [*off*] I want me Christmas presents.

LIZZIE: Go away, ugly cry-baby.

TOBY: [*off*] I never got my trike. I never saw my guinea pigs.

LIZZIE: Pissing your pants, scared of the dark –

TOBY: [*off, crying*] Where's mummy?

LIZZIE: Crying for mummy. She's forgotten all about you.

TOBY: [*off*] I'm lost.

LIZZIE: I'm going to prison. And I don't care.

TOBY: [*off*] When can I go home?

Panicked, she sings to her doll.

LIZZIE:

Hushabye, you naughty girl
Don't you make another peep.
No one worse in all the world.
Time to go to sleep.

A torch beam interrupts her. She crouches against the graffiti'd wall.

WARREN: [*off*] Lizzie?

WARREN *enters with a torch.*

You here, love?

He finds the doll and sleeping bag.

Lizzie!

He looks about.

Lizzie, I know you're here.

LIZZIE: Go away. This is my place.

WARREN: Where are you?

LIZZIE: Over the wall.

WARREN *looks up at the wall. He assumes she's on the other side.*

WARREN: Why'd you run away? Don't you like staying at my place?

Pause.

I want to talk to you.

LIZZIE: Well, I don't speak earth language, so you can't.

WARREN: What?

LIZZIE: Goffuloffuloffuloboloby.

WARREN: We haven't had a good natter for a while, have we? Not just us. Mum in the way, or stuff comes up on Saturday and / we don't have time to talk properly.

LIZZIE: Goffuloffuloffuloffolboloby!

WARREN: And I need to talk to you now, Lizzie! Will you come home, love?

LIZZIE: I live here.

WARREN: Do I have to climb over and get you?

LIZZIE: No-one can get over. It's my wall.

WARREN: It isn't safe here.

LIZZIE: I'm not scared of anything.

WARREN: I thought you were scared of the dark.

LIZZIE: I like the dark.

WARREN: [*quietly*] I don't know you any more. Where's my girl?

Silence.

Lizzie, you remember ... you know when you were little, and you'd get angry? ... I'd say, 'Go outside and bash up a tree', remember? And one time you came in with your fists all cut up. You said – you said to me, 'Dad, help me'.

Silence.

Please come home.

Silence.

I'm not going to play silly buggers. If you want a lift, I'm leaving. With or without you.

LIZZIE: I don't want anything.

WARREN: I'm not bluffing.

Pause.

And I'm not coming over to get you.

He jingles the car keys.

Righto. Leave you to the spooks then, eh?

Silence. Suddenly WARREN *hurls himself at the wall and beats against it.*

Lizzie!

LIZZIE *watches him. Fists bleeding,* WARREN *backs off.*

Damn you, then.

He exits. LIZZIE *returns to her doll and continues the song.*

LIZZIE:
No one knows you, no one cares.
You're not in your mother's prayers.
All you know to do is lie.
Hush, hushabye.

SCENE TWELVE

The police station. RAY *takes* ANGELA *and* WARREN *aside.* LIZZIE *stands apart.*

RAY: The thing is, I think she's on the brink of confessing. I know it looks rough, but it's the only way. If we let her off the hook, let her go home or have a sleep or anything, then we could lose her.

ANGELA: I'm so tired.

RAY: And I've just got a feeling that this is it. Now or never. She's been holding herself back. Every time she's about to tell me something she glances over at you and then she gives me some story.

WARREN: Right! That's our fault too, is it?

RAY: I just need you to do something. She's afraid of upsetting you. She doesn't want to make you angry.

Pause.

I want you to take her aside, and tell her you love her.

WARREN *laughs.*

And that, whatever happens, you'll be there for her. That all she has to do, to make you happy, is tell the truth.

ANGELA: I am so *tired.*

RAY: Can you do this for me?

WARREN: You want us to sit her down and say, 'If you want to make us happy, tell the policeman you're a murderer'!

ANGELA: What if she didn't?

RAY: The tests on her shoes / were positive –

ANGELA: Yes, but what if she didn't?

WARREN: She's 'sly and insolent'. It's obvious, isn't it!?

RAY: If she didn't, then she has nothing to confess. All we want is the truth. If you tell her it's alright to say what really happened that day, we might get it.

> WARREN *ignores* RAY. ANGELA *nods.* RAY *leaves.*

ANGELA: If there's nothing to tell, then let's just be sure of that. Let's just end it.

WARREN: My shift starts in a tick.

ANGELA: You're going to work?

WARREN: I've still got to pay your rent, yes!

ANGELA: Then let's get this over and done with. Please.

WARREN: This is a joke.

ANGELA: Don't make me do it alone.

WARREN: What are we making her say?

ANGELA: Just sit with me while I say it, then. Just hold her with me.

WARREN: We're making her put herself behind bars!

ANGELA: I'll tell her I'll be there, but *I* can't tell her you'll still love her.

> WARREN *finds his keys and starts to exit.*

WARREN: 'Course I love her. She's my daughter, isn't she?

ANGELA: I don't believe you're not going to help me.

WARREN: You've all gone mad. You do what your conscience can get away with, Angela. But don't try to pull me into it.

ANGELA: Warren! Listen, if that's what you think, then stop me!

WARREN: You always get your way. Why waste my breath?

ANGELA: Because she's your daughter!

> WARREN *stops.*

This is your last chance, Warren. My feelings are all numb. If I'm about to do something terrible, you've got to stop me.

WARREN: What'll you do if it's 'Yes'?

ANGELA: I don't know.

WARREN: Well, think about this. If Lizzie killed someone, whose fault is it?

ANGELA: Nobody's.

WARREN: Ours.

ANGELA: No ...

WARREN: Whatever way you look at it. If she was born that way, a monster, then it's something in us. You or me.

ANGELA: There's no such thing, no monsters.

WARREN: If it's all the other crap – how we brought her up – it's us. And we're going to get fried, either way. Christ, losing Lizzie is bad enough. But they're going to carve us up, Ange.

ANGELA: How can it be us? What have we done *wrong*?

WARREN: I did stuff at her age. The things other kids did to me, I shouldn't be alive to tell. I mean it.

Beat.

Maybe it's true.

ANGELA: What? What did you do?

WARREN: Oh, just stuff. Mad.

ANGELA: Tell me.

WARREN: Didn't you?

ANGELA: Yes. But we got away with it.

WARREN: We never hurt anyone.

ANGELA: *We* did.

WARREN: I mean, we never killed anyone.

ANGELA: I'd almost forgotten ...

WARREN: But it was just games. All kids did it. You had to.

ANGELA: Wanted to.

WARREN: Or you wouldn't have any friends. But we stopped in time.

ANGELA: Were stopped.

WARREN: Maybe she was just unlucky.

ANGELA: Yes.

WARREN: There's still time. Stop now. Save us.

ANGELA: I can't.

WARREN: Then I've only got one thing left to ask you. Is she my kid?

ANGELA: What?

WARREN: I'm not accusing you of anything. God knows I wish the answer was 'No'.

ANGELA: Did I screw around?

WARREN: I want to know if ... if I ever have kids again, with anyone ...
if it's me.

ANGELA: No, I didn't.

> WARREN *nods. He heads for the door.*

She might say 'No' ...

WARREN: What an anticlimax that'd be.

> WARREN *exits.* RAY *returns with* LIZZIE, *keeping her apart.*
> *He approaches* ANGELA. *She waves him away. She paces.*
> *He goes to her. They speak so* LIZZIE *can't hear.*

RAY: Then we can all go home.

ANGELA: But what if she didn't? What if she didn't?

RAY: Then that's what she'll say.

ANGELA: I shouldn't have brought her here.

RAY: Listen. You did the right thing.

ANGELA: How do you *know*?

RAY: Because I've seen Toby's mum and dad. They're ghosts, Angela.
Like every feeling has been drained out of them. You only have to
look at them and you know they'll never have a moment of joy
again, as long as they live. I don't know how they don't go mad
with grief. *Someone* did it, and they have to know why.

ANGELA: I'll never know a moment of joy again, either.

RAY: If she's guilty ... no.

> ANGELA *looks at* LIZZIE. *Then she nods for* RAY *to leave. He*
> *exits.* ANGELA *pulls* LIZZIE *into her lap.*

ANGELA: Lizzie. Whatever you did ... whatever happens ... all I want
is that you tell the truth. If you want to make mummy happy, just,
please, tell the truth. Because no matter what comes out of all this,
I love you, Lizzie. I know I haven't always been able to play with
you, or to give you things you wanted. And I haven't always done
everything right. I wish we could go back and I'd do it different.
But from this second on, for the rest of our lives, I promise you, I'll
be here.

LIZZIE: What about Dad?

ANGELA: Dad too. Just the same.

LIZZIE: Where is he?

ANGELA: He was just here. And the last thing he said was, he loves you more than anything.

LIZZIE: Why can't I go home?

ANGELA: They want the right answers.

LIZZIE: If I tell them 'Yes', can I go? Can I sleep?

> *For the first time* LIZZIE *cries, very softly.* ANGELA *rocks her, also crying.* RAY *enters.*

RAY: Okay then?

SCENE THIRTEEN

The police station. RAY *and* LIZZIE.

RAY: It is alleged that on Saturday, December the twenty-fourth, you were at the South-Star Shopping Mall. Is this correct?

LIZZIE: I'm in trouble, aren't I?

RAY: And while in the supermarket you attempted to lure away the toddler Toby Brian Chester from his mother.

LIZZIE: I never, he just started following me.

RAY: Did you take his hand? Don't nod your head.

LIZZIE: Yes, sir.

RAY: It is alleged that you then walked him a mile out of town to the vacant lot, which you call 'the weeds'. Is this correct?

LIZZIE: What's going to happen to me?

RAY: Is this correct?

LIZZIE: Yes, sir.

RAY: Did you or did you not asphyxiate Toby Brian Chester, causing death?

> *Silence.*

Shall I repeat the question?

> *Silence.*

Did you or did you not?

Silence.

I think you want to tell me you were playing with Toby.

LIZZIE *remains silent.*

I'm a reasonable bloke, Lizzie. I've been very patient with you. But it's wearing thin. I want a straight answer. I'm trying to do a job here. You're not making it easy for me. To be honest, I'm getting sick of the sight of you. Think I want another day of looking at your ugly mug? No. Well, do us all a favour.

LIZZIE *remains silent.*

This isn't a game. You're beginning to make me very angry, you are. All you have to do is say 'Yes'. Whatever it takes, I'm going to get it out of you. I don't care. I can stay here all night. All week. I'm not moving from this spot till I get an answer. By God. Oh, you think you're very smart, don't you, staring me out? Well I'm smarter than you, Miss Gael. I don't like your type. You've mucked me around long enough, your stories and smiles. You're a nasty piece of work. Sooner they put you away the better. Sooner your poor mum and dad see the back of you, we'll all be happier. And that won't be soon enough for me. Just give me an answer! I'm not leaving till I get a fucking ...

He raises his hand to strike her, but pulls back.

LIZZIE: 'Wolf', I said, 'Stop'. The Wolf was laughing and grinning like mad; I thought he was only playing. He never should've chucked that stone. But it was fun. He threw more. He got it on the leg, and made it bleed. It was going to make a big bruise. I said, 'Leave the baby now. Go home, Wolf!' But he was scared of getting busted. He said the baby would tell its mum and she'd kill us. He put his teeth on its throat. 'You just push up these two lumps in here', he said, 'and it'll never go home, we'll never get smacked.'

Pause.

Then we're walking home from the weeds, and the Wolf says, 'You know, you shouldn't have done that, Lizzie. You will get into ...'

Pause.

And I say, 'I never done anything!' [*Slowly*] And then he just stops, and says, 'Trouble'. And again he says, 'Trouble'.

They regard each other directly. A long moment. Blackout.

SCENE FOURTEEN

A garage. Semi-darkness. WARREN *rummages with a torch through a box of papers. He starts when* ANGELA *appears.*

ANGELA: Warren ... ?

WARREN: Just clearing out the last of my junk. You might want to park a car in here one day ...

ANGELA: I'm glad you're here. I never knew I could feel so alone.

He holds her.

WARREN: Thought I could make you breakfast.

ANGELA: They're keeping her there.

WARREN: Locked up? In a cell?

ANGELA: What happened to her, Warren? She was always chattering, wanting to know things, asking for cuddles ...

WARREN: Then suddenly there's a wall.

ANGELA: You know what I wish? That it was true. That if you looked you could see evil in her eyes, and she was born like that, and not because of us, but just because it happens.

WARREN: Yes ...

ANGELA: But I can't.

WARREN: No.

ANGELA: I can't bear it any more. I wish anything in the world had happened, but not this.

WARREN: There's still a chance.

ANGELA: But there's not. There's nothing.

WARREN: No.

ANGELA: Do you hate me?

WARREN: I'm trying. No.

ANGELA: Do something for me.

WARREN: Yes.

She beats her head against his chest.

ANGELA: Hit me. Hit me. Get the pain *out*!

WARREN: No.

ANGELA: I lied in that place last night. I told her I loved her.

WARREN: What?

ANGELA: Hit me!

WARREN: No!

> ANGELA *throws her head against him repeatedly. He shakes her.*

Stop it!

> *She goes limp.* WARREN *crushes her to him.*

We do. Love her. Ange.

ANGELA: Why didn't you switch the light on?

WARREN: I thought it was still busted. It was always busted. She's our kid!

ANGELA: Don't clear your stuff out.

WARREN: No.

ANGELA: I won't be getting a car. But you could keep the cab here. Between shifts.

WARREN: Yes. I could.

ANGELA: It'd be nice to be near each other again. Save paying two rents.

WARREN: I couldn't ever hate you.

ANGELA: So don't clear it out. Put it back. Bring it inside.

> *She goes to switch on the light.* WARREN *makes a vain attempt to stop her.*

WARREN: No ...

> *The light reveals the box of papers.*

ANGELA: What are you doing?

WARREN: I'd like that, Ange. I really would.

ANGELA: What's all that? Lizzie's things?

WARREN: I was looking. I miss her. Nothing.

ANGELA: Her school report.

WARREN: Just memories.

ANGELA: Her poems?

He wipes away his tears.

Warren. You're a bad liar.

WARREN: Just remembering things. Baby things.

ANGELA: What's it for?

WARREN: Don't. You won't understand.

ANGELA: Wait –

WARREN *starts to exit.*

WARREN: I'll go home for my stuff, then.

ANGELA: *Look* at me!

WARREN: Please ... / Don't ask me.

ANGELA: You're all I've got, Warren!

Beat.

WARREN: It's for all of us. I was going to tell you when I found out how much it was for. He said it'd be big. There'd be enough for *all* of us to finally move – go to the city or even the mainland.

ANGELA: You're going to sell this?

WARREN: And get her a decent lawyer, instead of some half-arsed uni drop-out the State gives you. She'd get off for sure. Then the rest of it we'd put in the bank for her. For when she's older. I could get my own cab. You could give up work. Look Ange, listen to me. This is all such a nightmare. It's unbearable, the worst hell anyone could ever go through. So if there's anything to get out of it at all, however small, anything / good –

ANGELA: The newspaper?

WARREN: Anything, then we should take it. It's like God's compo. It'd be stupid to knock it back. Ungrateful.

ANGELA: You sold the story. You're selling her drawings. The baby photos?

WARREN: I was going to ask you. Wait till after breakfast.

ANGELA: Oh God, Warren ...

WARREN: Poor and miserable, or rich and miserable. Our choice.

ANGELA: I can't look at you. I can't even look at you.

WARREN: Alright then! You tell me! You're such a saint, so high and mighty, always on your quest for Truth! You pull the bloody Truth out of our kid – *my* kid too, remember? And look where she's heading. I was going to come back? Live with you? You made up your mind and that was that. She's in a cell, for Christ's sake!

ANGELA: How many times did I ask you?

WARREN: There was no debate. Yeah, you asked me: asked me to make you feel alright about it.

ANGELA: You kept giving in. You kept vanishing.

WARREN: I had to think.

ANGELA: So did I. And at the same time I had to live with it all. Jesus Christ! *I don't believe you rang the papers!*

WARREN: They rang me.

ANGELA *shoves fistfuls of papers at* WARREN.

ANGELA: Just go! Go!

WARREN: Wait.

ANGELA *collapses.*

I want you to see something. She drew this in her book. It's a little boy. Lying with flowers all over him.

ANGELA: We loved each other once.

WARREN: She tried to show us this book. Remember?

ANGELA *turns away.*

You're right. You were right all along. I knew she did it. I just couldn't ...

WARREN *hesitates, then leaves the book open before her. He exits.*

SCENE FIFTEEN

A cell. LIZZIE *huddles in the corner, not looking at* RAY, *who sits with a newspaper, at a distance.*

RAY: Want anything? Book or anything?

LIZZIE *shakes her head.*

Very quiet over there.

LIZZIE *doesn't look up.*

Want the comics?

LIZZIE: No, thank you.

RAY: Where's your dolly today?

LIZZIE *shrugs.*

I bet you're a real little chatterbox with your mates. Don't you like me?

LIZZIE: Yes, sir.

RAY: Why so quiet, then?

LIZZIE: I don't want him to find me.

RAY: No one's allowed in here, don't you worry.

LIZZIE: He gets in.

RAY: You're locked up safe and sound. No one can get –

LIZZIE: He can slide under doors. And between the bricks.

RAY: Who?

LIZZIE: Shhh.

RAY: What does he look like?

LIZZIE: Big.

RAY: Big.

LIZZIE: Shhh. If he finds me, he'll never go away.

RAY: Someone'll be here round the clock, looking after you.

LIZZIE: You?

RAY: I've got to go home sooner or later.

LIZZIE: Why?

RAY: Well ... I've got my own kids. Got to see them, see my wife. Have a sleep.

LIZZIE: What about me?

RAY: Like I said: there'll be someone else after breakfast.

LIZZIE: Can I come home with you?

RAY *laughs uncomfortably.*

RAY: That's not allowed.

LIZZIE *gently rocks herself.*

Who gets in?

LIZZIE: The Wolf.

RAY: What does the Wolf do to you?

LIZZIE: He tries to swallow me.

RAY: He can't do that. You're a big strong girl.

LIZZIE: He did it before.

RAY: Did he?

LIZZIE: [*whispering*] At the weeds.

> RAY *approaches.*

RAY: Well, if we're very quiet, he won't find you here.

> LIZZIE *rocks herself.*

LIZZIE: What will they do to me?

RAY: Think about something else. It's not till tomorrow.

LIZZIE: I can't.

> *He holds her hand.*

Have you got any pets?

RAY: My son's got a ferret.

LIZZIE: I wish I could see it.

> *Pause.*

Maybe you could bring it after your breakfast.

RAY: Couldn't do that.

LIZZIE: I wouldn't hurt it.

RAY: I know.

LIZZIE: I promise I wouldn't.

> RAY *holds her.*

RAY: I know.

SCENE SIXTEEN

The house. ANGELA *packs* LIZZIE's *clothes.* RAY *watches her. He hands her an envelope.*

RAY: She wrote you a poem.

> ANGELA *puts it aside.*

Lucy Bell as Lizzie and Anthony Phelan as Ray in the 1996 Griffin Theatre production. Photo Robert McFarlane.

I wouldn't pack woollens. It'll be hot.

ANGELA: Winter'll come.

RAY: No. I mean, if ... if it happens, you know, they'll take care of all that. Wherever she goes.

Pause.

They still can't find a place willing to take her. It's an unusual case.

Pause.

Headlines don't help any.

He watches her pack.

You've still got tonight, if you want to see her. I could let you in.

ANGELA *shakes her head.*

She'd like to see you ...

ANGELA: Better not.

RAY *hands her* LIZZIE*'s sandals. Silence.*

RAY: She can't grasp it. I've explained the court system and all, how she's to respond to 'Child X'. But all she can talk about is having to wear broken shoes in court –

ANGELA: They're the best pair she's got. The others are no good for dresses.

RAY: And wetting the bed. She's very anxious about that.

Silence.

I've tried to make her understand that she may not be back. But she doesn't ... she keeps saying, 'When all this is over, I'm going to visit my Gran in Hobart'.

ANGELA *laughs.*

That's what the card's for. I said she might not be home for next Christmas. She asked could she write to you. It's just a cheap one I found in a drawer at the station.

Silence.

She's a funny kid.

Silence.

She's a lot like you.

ANGELA *keeps packing.*

Doesn't show much. Doesn't give much away. It's like there's a wall ...

ANGELA: That's her clothes. I'll send her school books on when I pick them up.

RAY: Walled herself in.

ANGELA: If you don't understand something, you don't know what to feel about it.

RAY: She never said she did it.

For the first time ANGELA *looks at him.*

The other things she admitted. But she never said the words, not about the little boy.

ANGELA: We know she did.

RAY: *We* do.

ANGELA: They tested the blood. The skin. Don't make me go over it.

RAY: It didn't have to come to this. That's all.

ANGELA: What?

RAY: As long as you feel you did the right thing.

ANGELA *stares at him.*

Because that's it, now.

ANGELA: What are you saying?

RAY: What do you think?

ANGELA: That I shouldn't have brought her to you?

RAY: It happens all the time, little kids getting killed and no one ever convicted.

ANGELA: What?

RAY: I'm not saying anything –

ANGELA: I – *What?*

RAY: Just –

ANGELA: Christ. No.

RAY *shrugs.*

From *you?*

RAY: Only that I hope you feel alright about it.

ANGELA: No! Of course I don't! I wish I was dead!

Tara Morice as Angela in the 1996 Griffin Theatre production. Photo Robert McFarlane.

RAY: Now now.

ANGELA: His parents. *They* needed to know. You said so!

RAY: I thought so. But what difference does it make? They'll never know why.

ANGELA: She could do it again. I don't know what goes on inside her head, how she sees things. I thought I did ... I don't know anything any more.

RAY: She could.

ANGELA: 'I murder so that I may come back'. She wrote it. She drew pictures. The shoes on the table. She took you to the place!

RAY: True.

ANGELA: She did it.

RAY: She wanted us to know.

ANGELA: How could I live with that? You can squash it down, but it never goes away. Watching her grow up, seeing her own kids, and always knowing.

RAY: She'd still have a life, at least.

ANGELA: But at what price? What would she have to block out, just to go from one day to the next? You'll never understand the choice I've had to make. Either way, her life is over: Living like that; or prison. It's the end. Either one will break her.

RAY: I didn't mean to upset you.

ANGELA *is silent. Then she gives him the suitcase.*

ANGELA: Say 'Hello' from me.

RAY: Will do.

ANGELA: And from her dad.

RAY: Yep.

ANGELA: Has he been in? To see her?

RAY: Nope.

ANGELA: Tell her we'll see her. On the day.

RAY: Anything else?

ANGELA: Tell me I was right.

RAY: 'Course you were.

He leaves. ANGELA *is motionless. Then she opens the card. She reads. The room goes dark, the Wolf appears.*

ANGELA: Go away. Oh please, go away!

Black.

SCENE SEVENTEEN

The Wolf's domain. LIZZIE *in a pinlight.*

LIZZIE: 'A Christmas Poem', by Lizzie Gael.
    I looked out the window tonight
    The moon and the stars were so bright!
    Then I heard a shout:
    'Help! Help! Let me out!'
    The voice was small
    It came from the wall
    It called to me further:
    'You know you'll do murder
    If you don't let me out.'

    Silence.

                    END

Hushabye

words by Hilary Bell

music by Phillip Johnston

Fine